ETHEREUM

The Definitive Guide to Investing in Ethereum and Blockchain Cryptocurrency

Artemis Caro

Copyright © 2017 Artemis Caro

All rights reserved.

INTRODUCING ETHEREUM

The year 2017 has seen a marked increase in general awareness and interest in digital currencies, such as Bitcoin, as well as the underlying technology driving this new economy, known as "blockchain." Major industries ranging from healthcare to finance, governmental agencies, and a wide variety of startups are beginning to explore the potential for blockchain technology to radically reshape the landscape of institutional structures.

There are generally two things that draw most people to the space of blockchain tech and cryptocurrencies. The first is money. Many people have heard the story of Bitcoin's rapid rise from having almost no value to being worth thousands of dollars over the course of a few short years. Naturally, everybody who hears about this today wishes that they had known about Bitcoin sooner and had invested in the early days. Of course, it makes sense that this would provoke anyone to look further into the cryptocurrency space in hopes of finding "another Bitcoin." This is how many people first become acquainted with Ethereum.

The second reason that people generally tend to be drawn to the cryptocurrency space is an interest in the technology. There is a great deal of potential for blockchain-based applications to reshape various industries, institutions, and social structures. Of course, these two broad interests, money and new technology, are not mutually exclusive. After all, who doesn't want to change the world *and* get rich at the same time?

Regardless of where your initial interest in

Ethereum comes from, it is important to understand Ethereum as both a currency and a technology. In this book, we will explore what this means and how Ethereum works, both as a digital asset and as a platform for building blockchain-based applications.

As we begin to explore Ethereum, it is important to note that many people refer to the Ethereum *currency* as "Ethereum." Technically, the currency unit is known as "Ether." Ether is one component of the much larger framework of "Ethereum." For the sake of clarity, we will use the term "Ether" in reference to the currency from now own, although in the real world you may see it called both Ether and/or Ethereum. As we progress through this book, the importance of recognizing the distinction between these two entities will become clearer.

Whether you plan to simply invest in Ether as a currency or you want to build a revolutionary application on the Ethereum platform, it is critical to understand the role of both the currency and the larger framework. In the cryptocurrency space, as of today, Ether is second only to Bitcoin in terms of popularity and value. In a few short years, it has gained considerable traction and become a forerunner in the burgeoning blockchain revolution.

Throughout this book, we will examine Ethereum's distinct approach to blockchain technology as a technological framework for building decentralized applications. We will cover what this means, how these applications work, and what you need to know if you're thinking about investing in Ether, a project built on the Ethereum platform, or even developing your own Ethereum-based application.

CONTENTS

	Introducing Ethereum	i
1	A Brief History of Ethereum	1
2	Overview of Blockchain Technology	5
3	The Ethereum Blockchain	9
4	Smart Contracts in Ethereum	11
5	The Ethereum Virtual Machine (EVM)	18
6	The Role of Ether in Smart Contracts	22
7	Consensus Algorithms: Proof-of-Work vs. Proof-of-Stake	26
8	Ethereum (eth) vs. Ethereum Classic (Etc)	30
9	Decentralized Applications Built on the Ethereum Platform	33
10	The Ethereum Enterprise Alliance (EEA)	37
11	Criticisms, risks & challenges concerning Ethereum	39
12	Getting started with Ethereum	44
13	The future of Ethereum, decentralized applications & blockchain Technology	49
	Conclusion	51

CHAPTER 1
A BRIEF HISTORY OF ETHEREUM

The initial concept for Ethereum was introduced in the year 2013, detailed in a white paper written by Russian-Canadian programmer Vitalik Buterin. Buterin, only 19 years old at the time, had already been was involved with Bitcoin for several years. In 2014, he received the Theil Fellowship and was awarded $100,000, which prompted him to go drop out of college and dedicate himself full-time to developing Ethereum.

As an active participant in the cryptocurrency space, Buterin saw the potential for extending the blockchain structure beyond Bitcoin. The initial vision for the Ethereum project was to create a platform to develop decentralized applications with broad capabilities. Simply put, Buterin envisioned possibilities for a Bitcoin-like system that could be used for more than just one kind of peer-to-peer financial transactions. Buterins ultimate vision for Ethereum can be viewed as an earnest attempt to apply learnings from Bitcoin's decentralized, global cryptographic network to challenges beyond mere value exchange. Rather than just cutting out the middle man and simply sending and receiving money, the programmers saw the bigger picture and saw the possibility of using "bitcoins" to represent commodities, derivatives or even deeds to real estate – Pretty much anything for which a secure, fixed unit of code could function as a digital asset.

In essence, Buterin envisioned how the platform could remove the conventional arbitrators of trust and in turn enable a new wave of application development – one that could possibly change the way we carry out "trusted" transactions without the use of outdated, painstaking slow legal systems that are in place today.

By 2014, Ethereum had established a core team of developers, gained considerable support, and was officially under development. A crowd-sale of the initial round of Ether, the digital currency used by Ethereum, took place in July-August of 2014, with proceeds funding further development of the software.

On July 30, 2015, the first iteration of Ethereum officially went live. Today, Ethereum is still maintained by a central team of developers, including founder Vitalik Buterin, and is managed by a Swiss non-profit organization called the Ethereum Foundation. Unlike Bitcoin, whose creator remains a mystery, Buterin serves as a figurehead for this project and his identity is very much tied to Ethereum. While there are many other programmers and thinkers contributing to the development of Ethereum, Buterin is generally viewed as the inventor and the "face" of the project. Some critics have expressed concern over the centrality of the Ethereum project and a "cult of personality" surrounding Buterin.

Throughout its short history, Ethereum has provoked international interest, gained a lot of support, and received its fair share of criticism, as well. Ether, as a currency, despite periods of volatility, has become one of the more valuable digital currencies in the cryptocurrency space.

Particularly because it is such a new technology, it is impossible to predict what the future holds for the Ethereum platform. Throughout 2016 and 2017, we have seen a huge uptick in global interest in cryptocurrencies and the concept of blockchain technology across many industries and institutions. The Ethereum platform represents, for many, the closest thing that currently exists to a framework for building decentralized blockchain applications capable of running autonomously. At the same time, Ethereum is still in its early stages. Many argue that it has not yet reached the level of stability, security and scalability necessary to usher in the future of blockchain and decentralized applications.

Throughout this book, we will explore the capabilities, potential, and challenges presented by Ethereum. We will take a broad look at the concepts and practical applications of this new technology. It is important to understand that many of the underlying aspects of Ethereum, particularly when looking at critiques and the roadmap for development, are highly technical.

While getting into the code itself and many of the mathematical concepts under the hood of the Ethereum platform is beyond the scope of this book, we will zoom in on the foundational ideas and explore the practical questions:

What is it? How does it work? How can I use it? We will explore the fundamental differences between Bitcoin and Ethereum, and look at some real-world examples of how Ethereum is being used to develop new kinds of applications.

CHAPTER 2
OVERVIEW OF BLOCKCHAIN TECHNOLOGY

Before we begin to dig into the specifics of Ethereum, it is crucial to understand some of the core principles of blockchain technology, in general. For newcomers to the cryptocurrency space, one of the concepts that can be initially quite confusing is the relationship between cryptocurrencies and blockchain.

Blockchain technology is the underlying force behind both Bitcoin and Ethereum, but these two projects use this technology in different ways. To understand how Ethereum implements the blockchain, however, it is helpful to have some background in Bitcoin.

Bitcoin was the first digital currency *and* the first application built on a blockchain platform. Today, Bitcoin is by far the most popular and well-known cryptocurrency, as well as the largest, active open blockchain in the world. As Bitcoin began to enter into the mainstream, many media outlets developed a tendency to (incorrectly) use the terms "Bitcoin" and "blockchain" almost interchangeably. Even today, many articles can be found that struggle to clearly elucidate the relationship between Bitcoin, other cryptocurrencies, and blockchain technology.

For the sake of clarity, let's break down the fundamentals. Bitcoin is fundamentally a currency. It was designed to enable digital, secure, peer-to-peer financial transactions and it has been, for the most part, highly successful in achieving this specific goal. Bitcoin uses a blockchain to perform its function. Blockchain technology, on the other hand, has implications that extend far beyond Bitcoin, and far beyond the realm of digital currencies, in general.

The blockchain model upon which Bitcoin is built works very well for Bitcoin, albeit with some areas for improvement. (For example, Bitcoin transactions can take a long time to be approved, which presents a barrier to entry for many merchants in terms of accepting payment in Bitcoin. Nobody wants to wait around in a store for an hour while a Bitcoin transaction is being verified).

While Bitcoin was the first technology to implement the blockchain, early adopters, like Vitalik Buterin, quickly began to see the potential for blockchain architecture in a wide variety of other environments. Because Bitcoin was designed specifically to be a currency, innovators began to explore the question of whether the particular blockchain structure employed by Bitcoin was the best model upon which to build other applications, beyond peer-to-peer transactions of a digital currency. Ethereum was born from this idea of creating a more flexible environment for deploying the power of blockchain technology in a universal way, across a broad spectrum of different applications.

So, what is a blockchain is and how does it work? To truly answer this question in depth would require trudging through some fairly advanced mathematical concepts that are a bit beyond the scope of this book. Fortunately, unless you plan on becoming a programmer, you don't really need to understand the nitty-gritty of cryptographic hashing algorithms in order to get a solid grasp of the broader concepts and structure of blockchain.

Blockchains do use complex math, but if we zoom out they are ultimately fairly simple to understand from a bird's eye view. Starting with the terminology, we have "blocks" that are linked together, one after another, to form a "chain." Each block is made up of some kind of *data* related to events that took place during a particular period of time. The most recent block contains data pertaining to the most recent events. In the case of Bitcoin, this data is transaction data, such as the addresses of the Bitcoin wallets sending and receiving funds, the amount of coin being transacted, the time of the transactions, and other such details.

So, each new block is a collection of a bunch of data about the most recent transactions that have taken place. Each block is linked to the previous block with a special kind of cryptographically secure time stamp. Some complex math stuff happens here to make sure that *any new block matches up with the entire history of all previous transactions on the entire blockchain.*

Each new timestamp must match up with the previous block's timestamp, which in turn linked to the one before that, thus creating a long chain where each block is verifiably connected to the previous one, all the way back to the very first block, known as the "genesis block." The entire history of every single Bitcoin transaction that has ever occurred is recorded on the blockchain, which is publicly available for anyone to look at. The potential for secure transactions with this level of transparency is a feature that has drawn many people to

Bitcoin and to blockchain technology.

Simply put, the Bitcoin blockchain is ultimately just a record of every single verified Bitcoin transaction that has ever happened. Transactions that happen in a given period of time are grouped together in blocks. Multiple, identical copies of the blockchain are stored and updated constantly by a big network of participating computers all over the world. This is what is known as a "distributed ledger." A distributed ledger is fundamentally just a giant decentralized database, or a record of information, events or transactions. Decentralization is a core concept behind the blockchain architecture of both Bitcoin and Ethereum, as well as many other blockchain-based initiatives and cryptocurrencies.

Not all distributed ledgers are blockchains, but *all blockchains use some kind of distributed ledger system.* Usually, this means that identical copies are stored and updated simultaneously on many different machines all over the world. In the case of Bitcoin, for anyone to hack or "cheat" the blockchain, they would have to manipulate the data of not only one block, but the *entire historical record,* on the majority of the entire network of decentralized machines, all at the same time. The kind of computational power required to do this makes it virtually impossible under current conditions, thus making the system secure by design.

Conceptually, while not totally identical, the Ethereum blockchain is structured in much the same way. The fundamental difference, when looking at Ethereum, is the *kind* of data that is being stored in blocks and the *way that data is handled.*

CHAPTER 3
THE ETHEREUM BLOCKCHAIN

Today, Bitcoin continues to be the largest, open public blockchain and serve as the definitive model upon which many other blockchain-based applications are based. However, the Bitcoin blockchain is only one implementation of blockchain technology. As more and more industries begin to explore the potential of blockchain, new models are emerging on a regular basis, often suited to serve a specific purpose.

When we look at Bitcoin, we see that fundamentally its purpose is a decentralized, peer-to-peer digital currency. Bitcoin solves a particular problem: how to make secure financial transactions on a peer-to-peer basis from anywhere in the world while eliminating the need for trust, a middleman, or centralized authority like a bank. While Bitcoin is not perfect, it has been quite successful in terms of serving the purpose for which it was intended.

As developers and entrepreneurs began to see implications for blockchain technology that went far beyond financial transactions, many began to imagine alternative blockchain structures that might be more suited to accomplish different functions. Vitalik Buterin, the developer who invented Ethereum, envisioned an open platform upon which anybody could build a blockchain-based application to perform any kind of function.

Rather than a blockchain that simply stored

financial transaction data, as with Bitcoin, the Ethereum blockchain is designed to execute code based on verified transactions. Instead of simply moving funds from Account A to Account B, as with Bitcoin, Ethereum could create an environment where a transaction from Account A to Account B could trigger a vast range of events. For example, transactions in Ethereum can be used to register a new domain name, transfer property titles, manage voter registration, or execute secure contracts between two or more parties. In fact, "transactions" within Ethereum are often referred to as "smart contracts."

CHAPTER 4
SMART CONTRACTS IN ETHEREUM

The term "Smart Contracts" comes up a lot in reference to Ethereum. What is a smart contract? The short answer is that a smart contract is a computer program. Smart contracts are really the "meat and potatoes" of Ethereum, and it is worth exploring this concept in some depth in order to really grasp the power and vision of the platform.

If you don't have much in the way of technical background, don't worry. When it comes to actually *writing* smart contracts you will need to learn to code or hire a programmer, but you don't need to know how to code in order to understand, conceptually, how smart contracts work. However, it is helpful to have a basic understanding of how computer programs work, even if you don't necessarily know how to write them yourself.

While they can do incredibly complex things, all computer programs essentially work by asking a series of yes or no questions. When we think about all "data" ultimately consisting of 1's and 0's, or binary code, what those 1's and 0's represent are "yes's" and "no's". Broadly speaking, there are no "maybes" for a computer. If we could write a simple computer program in English, it might look something like this:

Dear computer, if I am playing a video and I click the pause button, then please pause the video.

In this example, the computer will first need to check if I am playing a video. This is the first "yes or no" question it will need to answer. If the answer is "yes," I am playing a video, then it will ask question number two: am I clicking the pause button? Let's say I'm not. For as long as I am playing the video (i.e. as long as the first answer is still "yes"), the computer will wait, patiently, asking that second question over and over again until the answer is "yes." It's only mission in life, as long as I am playing a video, is to check constantly whether or not I am pressing the pause button. As soon as I do press the pause button, the answer to the second question becomes "yes," and then it will pause the video.

When we think about digital transactions happening with Bitcoin, what we're really doing when we participate in these transactions is executing a simple computer program. The essence of what happens is that Person A sends funds to Person B. Bitcoin's software will ask a series of questions: Does Person A actually have sufficient funding? Can Person A verify ownership of the address holding those funds? Is the address for Person B valid? As long as the correct inputs are provided, the decentralized Bitcoin network will reach a consensus for performing the computations and executing the program: the transaction will be verified and Person B will receive the funds.

With Bitcoin, the program that is running *only deals with one type of transaction*. "Bitcoins" are essentially just numbers that are moved around from one digital address to another, and the record of all of those moves is stored on the blockchain. The blockchain provides a system for a decentralized network of computers to reach a consensus about which tasks to perform and then to perform said tasks. In the case of Bitcoin, the "tasks" are transfers of coin from Person A to Person B, but is there any reason why this system couldn't be used to handle other types of tasks? Well, no, and that is precisely what Ethereum is built to do. Ethereum uses the same blockchain infrastructure, but it opens the door for *any type of program* to be executed.

Even when we continue to think in terms of financial transactions, the possibilities that Ethereum offers allow for things like conditions, creating a much more flexible environment for payment systems. For example, with Ethereum, a secure deposit could be held on the blockchain for a specified period of time: if a set of conditions were not met, it could be returned to the payer; if the conditions were met, the payment could be released to the payee. In Bitcoin, there is no way to hold a payment in "escrow" like this without the use of a third party. This kind of conditional transaction is a simple example of something that could be executed with a smart contract in Ethereum.

Another use case for smart contracts could include a 'multi-signature' approach to releases funds, meaning that a specified number of people must all agree to release the funds in order for the contract to be fulfilled. To further complicate matters, but also make them much more exciting, smart contracts are actually often used to trigger *other* smart contracts. For example, let's say you wanted to place a bet that your favorite sports team was going to win their next game: You could use one contract to place the bet, and in the background another smart contract would be used to gather data about the game and process the results, which would then send the outcome back to yet another smart contract to handle dispensing payout to the winner.

As we become more integrated into the Internet of Things, smart contracts open up a whole world of possibilities. For example, as smart cars become more prevalent, we could easily envision a transition from the old system of needing to put money in a parking meter to a system that would run entirely on smart contracts. Sensors could easily link specific cars to specific parking spaces, and a smart contract could be used to automatically deduct the appropriate fee based on the time a car was parked in a given space. Rather than digging around for change under the seat and dealing with parking meters, drivers could just park and the smart contract would manage the transaction in the background. Cities could do away with the entire system of meter maids and automate the entire process.

The concept of a supply chain can also serve as a good example for visualizing how smart contracts can be linked together in a real-world scenario. Let's say you go to a store and buy a toothbrush. This store normally only has 10 of these toothbrushes in stock, and you buy the last one. Many more are housed at a warehouse 100 miles away. They are manufactured, however, in China. The chemical plant that supplies the plastic to make this toothbrush is actually located in Texas.

At the point of exchange, when you buy the toothbrush, a network of smart contracts could immediately inform the warehouse that the store needs more inventory, which would in turn inform the manufacturer that they will need to get another shipment ready for the warehouse, which will in turn let the plastic supplier know that, in order to make more toothbrushes, the factory in China will need to have more raw materials shipped over to them.

The advantages to automating this entire system via smart contracts include eliminating a huge amount of paperwork, bureaucracy, delay time, human error, and fees associated with middlemen required in each instance to physically contact the next link up in the supply chain and negotiate each order. Making these incredibly complex systems more efficient and less vulnerable to corruption by creating a transparent record of every transaction is one of the most promising applications for smart contracts.

Despite the fundamental differences between Bitcoin and Ethereum, many people tend to treat these two projects as "competitors," battling for control of the blockchain space. Even for those who are only interested in Ether as a currency, and don't care particularly about the technology, this mindset is not really accurate. Ultimately, Bitcoin and Ethereum are two distinct, coexisting technologies that have different goals and applications. Bitcoin is designed to be a currency: it is an end in and of itself. Ethereum utilizes Ether as a way to execute smart contracts: the Ether currency is a means to end. In this sense, the two projects are not really competitors, in that they both have different visions, goals, and uses.

In order to further grasp the concept of smart

contracts, and how the Ethereum platform works, it is useful to explore some of the fundamentals of software development. If you have some experience working with any programming language, you will have an advantage in terms of understanding the way that code is executed using smart contracts. If not, don't worry. Again, you don't actually need to know how to write code in order to understand how Ethereum works, but it is useful to become familiar with some basic programming concepts.

Understanding the Concept of "State" in Applications

Within software development, there is a concept known as "state." Very basically, state refers to what is happening within an application at any given moment in time. Whenever something changes, that application's state changes.

For example, imagine you are visiting a web page that requires you to sign up for an account. You would most likely need to fill in a form with some information and click a "Submit" button to send your form to the website's server. You would then be taken to a "Welcome" page and given access to rest of the website. Behind the scenes, when you send in the form and the website takes you to the Welcome page, the *state* of the program being executed on the website changes.

Why does this matter? Smart contracts in Ethereum are ultimately programs or applications. Each iteration of an application's state is stored on the blockchain. This might sound complicated- and it is, in fact, pretty complicated- but this record of a program's history is fundamental to how smart contracts work in

Ethereum. Within Ethereum applications, when a "transaction" occurs, software code can be triggered and executed. Thus, the state of that application can be changed and a record of what happened within the code is stored on the blockchain. By maintaining this record, the entire history of any given application's execution can be accessed and used to verify claims and regulate transactions.

CHAPTER 5
THE ETHEREUM VIRTUAL MACHINE (EVM)

All of the machines participating in the Ethereum network are called "nodes." Much like Bitcoin and other decentralized peer-to-peer networks, there are many nodes spread out all across the world. Anybody can choose to run a node. In terms of Ethereum, we can think of all of these different computers merging together, in a sense, to form one giant computer capable of performing distributed computations. This concept is known as the "Ethereum Virtual Machine," often abbreviated to EVM.

Virtual machines (or VM's), in computing terms, are emulated computer systems. If you've ever partitioned your hard-drive to run both Windows and OSX, you've used one kind of virtual machine. For our purposes, we don't really need to know too much about the role of virtual machines, in general. When it comes to the Ethereum Virtual Machine, the thing that is important to know is that it is the *runtime environment* for smart contracts. Each node on the Ethereum network runs an implementation of the EVM.

Like most virtual machines, the Ethereum Virtual Machine works at a very low-level, meaning that it processes code written in a "low-level" programming language. For developers, writing smart contracts is a lot more efficient when done in a "high-level" language. So, smart contracts are written in one language, usually

Solidity, and then compiled (using a special program called a "compiler") into the low-level code that can be processed by the EVM environment.

Smart contracts run on the Ethereum Virtual Machine, which runs on each participating node. When we consider what we know about blockchain technology and what we have just covered concerning Ethereum, a few questions may arise.

First, if every instance of an application's state is stored on the blockchain, doesn't that mean the blockchain will become really, really big? Won't that make it difficult for nodes to continuously maintain it? How can smaller nodes use the network efficiently if they don't have the capacity to store the entire state? Good question!

If the Ethereum blockchain used the same approach and structure as Bitcoin- that is, if it simply recorded a long list of every single thing ever that happened with every application- it would indeed create problems in terms of efficiency and scalability. As you may have guessed, this is not exactly how it works.

In fact, this is one of the facets of the Ethereum blockchain that makes it unique, diverging from the architecture of the original blockchain as implemented by Bitcoin. Ethereum uses a particular kind of data structure based on a mathematical principle called a Merkle Tree. Bitcoin's blockchain also uses a Merkle Tree, but to get technical, Ethereum actually uses a special kind of Merkle Tree known as a Merkle Patricia Tree.

The Merkle Patricia Tree used by Ethereum is a way of storing data (i.e. the data that makes up the "blocks") as a set of key/value pairs. A "key" is a short code that corresponds to a specific "value," which can be a much longer piece of data.

These keys and values are generated and authenticated using cryptographically secure algorithms. Keys and values can only be generated in one very specific way using a particular mathematical method that only works in one-direction. What this means is that any data (the value) that is fed into the algorithm will result in the same key every time. However, you cannot reverse the process by feeding a key into the system to arrive at the initial value.

Given the same set of keys and values, you would get the exact same Merkle Tree structure each and every time. Even a slight change in one bit of input data will yield a completely different output. Conceptually, this is the most important detail to grasp in terms of how verification works: *any data that you feed into the algorithm will generate the identical cryptographically secure output each time as long as the data remains unchanged.*

Thus far, what we have described is pretty much the same aspect of Merkle Trees that are used in the Bitcoin blockchain. What makes Ethereum's model different is the "Patricia" part of the Merkle Patricia Tree. This has to do with how the keys are positioned throughout the blockchains data structure.

Getting into the mathematical logic behind the scenes is a bit beyond the scope of this book, but broadly speaking the system is able to decide how to merge and arrange data stored in blocks by using prefixes that are assigned to each key. What this means, practically speaking, is that nodes have the ability to verify authenticity without needing to download the entire blockchain.

In fact, individual nodes will almost never need to access the entire state of the system to perform a given computation. Downloading the entire blockchain, therefore, would not be very efficient. Instead, a node can download only the partial state that it needs, and it can verify that chunk of code (or that "branch of the tree") by checking it, using the keys, against the surrounding branches. Because the surrounding branches will contain a reference linked all the way back to the root (the very first transaction), nodes can verify the partial state without needing to download the entire state history. This makes transactions in Ethereum much faster, more efficient, and allows for greater scalability of the platform.

CHAPTER 6
THE ROLE OF ETHER IN SMART CONTRACTS

Smart contracts, we have learned, are computer programs, or "scripts," written in code. These scripts are written in a Turing-complete programming language. "Turing-complete," by definition, means that this language is capable of doing any kind of computation. If something can be expressed with an algorithm, a Turing-complete language can express it. While there are a few languages that can be used to write smart contracts, the most popular today is called Solidity. Solidity is similar in many ways to JavaScript, a very versatile and widely used programming language notable for its use in web applications.

One major problem posited by Turing-complete machines (i.e. any machine capable of running scripts written in a Turing-complete language) is known as the "halting problem." Basically, what this means is that the computer has no way of knowing in advance whether a program will stop at some point, or if it will loop forever and ever and ever (in programming terms, this is known as an "infinite loop"). The only way to determine this is by actually running the code.

For example, imagine I had a program that said something like: "Dear computer, please give me a random number." While it is possible that I could get a number like 50 or 300, you might also notice that I did not specify a length. It is entirely possible that the computer would spit out a number so long that, if unchecked, it could go on and on and on towards infinity. A better idea might be to tell the computer, "Dear computer, please give me a random number less than 1000." Then, of course, it could spit out a negative number that headed on towards infinity. So, I might tell it, "Ok, fine, please give me a random number between 0 and 1000." The poor computer is just trying to do its job, but this time it might spit out a number like 1.500000… followed by infinite 0's. Really, to get our program to work, we would need to specify that we want a whole number, or integer, between 0 and 1000.

Getting programs to run the way we want them to is not always easy, and it is not uncommon for programming bugs to lead inadvertently to "infinite loops." A machine has no way of knowing whether or not it will run into an infinite loop in a piece of code until it actually runs that code, at which point it is stuck. If any node on the Ethereum network got stuck running a program in an infinite loop, it would effectively halt the entire system, hence being called "the halting problem." This inability to complete a script would stop new data from being added to the blockchain. That would, obviously, be bad. So, how can we avoid this problem?

The answer is actually pretty simple: Ether. Within the Ethereum network, computation is not free. Every time a user makes a request to run a script, a certain fee is associated, which is paid in Ether. Furthermore, in order to run a script, a user must set a limit to the amount of Ether put towards running that script. The Ether dedicated to running a particular script is known as "gas." If the script runs out of Ether, or "gas", before completion, it will simply halt at its current state.

By requiring a fee and forcing a value cap to be set for each script, Ethereum eliminates the problem of infinitely looping programs, be they accidental, or, as is more likely the case, malicious denial-of-service attacks. Nobody has an infinite amount of Ether, so even if a bad actor attempted to execute an infinitely looping program they would not be able to sustain the funding required to continue running the program. The script would be cut off from executing as soon as the funding ran out.

Ether, as a currency, plays an integral role in the Ethereum framework. Outside of usage as "gas" towards executing smart contracts on the Ethereum blockchain, however, Ether is also traded on many popular exchanges for other cryptocurrencies and some fiat currencies, like dollars and euros.

In the US you can buy Ether with fiat currency through several digital currency exchanges, including Coinbase, Bittrex, and others. You can buy Ether with Bitcoin through almost all notable exchanges, including ShapeShift, Kraken, Poloniex, and more. Depending on where you are in the world, your access to specific exchanges will vary, but you should have no trouble buying, selling, or trading Ether through one or more online platforms no matter where you live.

Ether has a significant real-world value beyond the role of "gas." One Ether has reached a value of over $300 at several periods throughout 2017. For many, Ether is treated exclusively as an investment, with speculators exchanging Bitcoin or other digital currencies for Ether in hopes that the value of Ether will increase. If it does, they may simply trade their Ether back into fiat without ever really engaging with any applications on the Ethereum network. In this sense, Ether can be bought, sold, and traded like Bitcoin or any other digital currency. Within the Ethereum framework, however, Ether serves a unique purpose as "gas" for running smart contracts.

Even if your interest in Ethereum is purely as a financial investment and you don't plan on writing software or being involved in any way with applications built on the platform, it is helpful to understand the relationship between those applications, the structure of the Ethereum ecosystem, and the value of Ether as a currency.

We know that Ether can be bought on various currency exchanges, but where does Ether actually come from? Who makes it and how? As of the time of this writing, Ether is "mined" in a manner similar to Bitcoin. Nodes in the Ethereum network perform complex math problems in order to validate transactions. When a particular node, or miner, successfully "solves a block," that block is added to the blockchain and the miner is rewarded for their work with a certain amount of Ether. This structure may be changing in the near future, however, and it leads us to another important concept.

We need to look a bit more closely at the role of mining, how transactions are validated, how the blockchain is maintained, and how this relates to the future of Ethereum.

CHAPTER 7
CONSENSUS ALGORITHMS: PROOF-OF-WORK VS. PROOF-OF-STAKE

A significant part of what drives the real-world implementation of blockchain protocols involves conducting secure transactions, whether they are purely financial transactions as with Bitcoin or whether they are transactions of other types of information or data. When one party sends information to another, how does the system guarantee that the information is valid?

We have touched already on the concept of a distributed ledger, and the role of decentralized networks in maintaining a blockchain. As a practical matter, what this means is that many people all over the world need to run software that validates transactions and records those transactions to the blockchain. In some cases, this can get quite expensive in terms of both computer power and electricity. To encourage people to participate, we can imagine that they might need some incentive. This is where "mining" comes in.

Bitcoin miners notoriously require specialized equipment that performs thousands of complex mathematical operations every second. These calculations eat up significant processing power and consume a lot of electricity. We will not go too in depth into how Bitcoin mining works, specifically, but the general idea is that miners compete to solve a complex math problem in order to validate each new block that is added to the blockchain.

The solution to the problem, each time, is basically a random number, and the only way to find it is by trial and error. So, miners use their equipment to try out tons of random numbers as quickly as possible until they find one that matches the criteria set forth by the core code of the Bitcoin software. When a miner thinks they have found a solution, they broadcast this to the entire Bitcoin network and other miners check their solution. When a majority of miners agrees that the solution is correct, the block is added to the blockchain and the miner who found the solution is rewarded with brand new Bitcoin that are generated from the Bitcoin software. For active miners, the potential for earning the reward outweighs the cost incurred by running mining equipment, which encourages participation in the system.

This model is known as "Proof-of-Work." Because the only way to solve the problem required to validate a block is via trial and error, there is no way for a miner produce a correct result and get the reward other than by doing the work of computation.

Like Bitcoin, Ethereum has historically worked on a "Proof-of-Work" consensus model. However, in early 2017 it was announced that Ethereum intends to shift towards implementing a "Proof-of-Stake" consensus model in the near future. Vitalik Buterin, Ethereum's creator, released a whitepaper in May of 2017 proposing the implementation of a new Proof-of-Stake algorithm called Casper into the Ethereum protocol. The timeframe remains unclear, but early reports suggest that the Casper algorithm will be phased in over time. Ethereum enthusiasts have met this news with mixed feelings, and there is ongoing speculation as to how Proof-of-Stake will translate into real-world applications.

In order to understand how this might impact Ethereum, let's explore how Proof-of-Stake generally works. When looking at Proof-of-Work, we saw that there is a real-world cost associated with performing what are essentially meaningless calculations in order to find a random number to solve a block and claim a reward. To get a sense of how significant this cost is, it is estimated that both Bitcoin and Ethereum eat up over $1 million *per day* in electricity and hardware costs associated with mining.

Ethereum's proposed Proof-of-Stake (PoS) model eliminates the resource drain presented by PoW. Rather than relying on miners, participants in this model take on the role of "validators." Similar to placing a bet, validators stake a certain amount of their own Ether towards solving a block. The higher the amount a validator stakes, the greater the probability that they will solve the block. If they "win," they will be rewarded.

In the event that a bad actor attempts to manipulate the system, their stake will simply disappear out of circulation. The Ether they have put towards attempting to validate a false transaction, for example, will be eliminated from the total amount of Ether in existence. In theory, this will increase the overall value of the currency due to the principle of scarcity. In economics, the scarcity principle basically implies that where there is demand, the less of commodity there is, the greater its value.

The Casper algorithm represents a new model for implementing Proof-of-Stake consensus in a real-world environment. Among Ethereum users and throughout the larger cryptocurrency and blockchain community, there is much ongoing debate over PoW versus PoS, both generally and in relation to Ethereum, specifically.

If successful, some of the advantages of Proof-of-Stake include the aforementioned elimination of resource consumption required for mining, and potentially a greater level of security and scalability. Faster transactions speeds may also be a result. However, until the Casper algorithm is implemented, many of these possibilities remain theoretical, and many skeptics maintain the attitude of, "I'll believe it when I see it."

As a platform for handling smart contracts, Ethereum opens up the potential of blockchain technology for a wide variety of applications by creating a secure, hack-proof, trustless environment for creating and executing smart contracts. Fundamental to this platform is the way in which transactions of information are validated, and validation is handled by the consensus algorithm. Consensus algorithms are a big deal in terms of the functionality of a decentralized blockchain environment. Naturally, there are those who are apprehensive and have concerns about how shifting the consensus algorithm from Proof-of-Work to Proof-of-Stake may impact Ethereum. Some, of course, believe that Proof-of-Stake will present a positive evolution in terms of improving the efficiency of the blockchain architecture.

Will Proof-of-Stake actually perform as intended when implemented in the real world? The answer remains to be seen, but for those with a vested interest in Ethereum, this is an important space to watch moving forward.

CHAPTER 8
ETHEREUM (ETH) VS. ETHEREUM CLASSIC (ETC)

For those who are in the early stages of discovering the cryptocurrency space, one hurdle that may catch the eye is the existence of Ethereum Classic, abbreviated as ETC on many popular exchanges and cryptocurrency tickers. What is the difference between Ethereum and Ethereum Classic?

If you aren't confused enough already, in order to understand Ethereum Classic it is necessary, also, to become familiar with The DAO. DAO, in general, stands for "decentralized autonomous organization." *The DAO* was a specific decentralized autonomous organization that was launched on the Ethereum blockchain in 2016. The DAO was designed to offer a model for a new kind of institutional structure, useful for both businesses and non-profit organizations. This particular venture issued a token sale in May of 2016 as a way to crowd-fund development. This token sale was very successful and raised around $150-million in under a month. Then, The DAO's code was hacked just one month later, in June of 2016. Hackers used a known vulnerability in the code to reallocate around one-third of the money into a different account, valued at around $50 million at the time of the attack.

In July of 2016, after the hack, there was a decision within the Ethereum community to "hard-fork" the blockchain. A "fork" in a blockchain is much a like a fork in a road- a split, where one path becomes two. In the case of Ethereum, hard-forking the blockchain made it possible to go back and recover the stolen funds and return them to The DAO.

The DAO hard-fork created a large dispute within the Ethereum community. A significant number of participants in the network were against splitting the blockchain, and as a result, they continued to maintain the pre-forked chain. The pre-forked version of the blockchain became Ethereum Classic. The other members of the Ethereum network moved over to the new blockchain, which continued on as Ethereum. Since then, Ethereum has forked a few more times in response to other attacks, strengthening its defenses against DDoS attacks and spamming in the meantime. The subsequent forks were not nearly as controversial and did not spawn "competing versions" of Ethereum.

There continues to be an ongoing debate within the Ethereum community over the role of Ethereum Classic and the larger politics surrounding blockchain forks. There are some who are ideologically opposed to the idea of forking, no matter what, arguing that the inherent value and guiding principle of a blockchain are that it cannot be altered. Others believe that forking can be a necessary, acceptable, and useful way for blockchain projects to adapt in response to changing circumstances, technological advances, and user demands.

Debate exists concerning investment viability as well as ideology. There are those who will assert that Ethereum Classic is "dead," and those who believe it will ultimately overtake Ethereum as the dominant "fork" of the blockchain, the latter of which are a minority. Looking at the history of both in terms of their respective currencies, it is safe to say that the majority of investors seem to trend, thus far, towards Ethereum rather than Ethereum Classic.

CHAPTER 9
DECENTRALIZED APPLICATIONS BUILT ON THE ETHEREUM PLATFORM

We've talked about Ethereum as a platform for building decentralized applications (dApps), but we haven't really explored what these look like in much depth. Bearing in mind, once again, that this technology has only existed for a few years, we have already seen a number of very interesting projects emerge that are built on top of the Ethereum architecture.

The focus of this book is primarily on Ethereum, itself, but it is worth looking at some of the ways this platform has been implemented in different applications and real-world scenarios.

One of the core features of Ethereum is that it allows anyone to issue their own digital token or currency. Ether is used as "gas" to finance the execution of smart contracts within the Ethereum ecosystem. Applications built on top of Ethereum's code base, but suited towards performing a specific function, may choose to create their own token to use as "gas" within their particular blockchain ecosystem.

One example to illustrate this concept is the Golem project. Golem is one of the most well established and widely known applications build on the Ethereum framework, and it has its own currency, also called Golem (GNT).

The general idea behind Golem is to create a

platform for decentralized computing. Lots of people have computers. Most people don't really use their computers to their full capacity all of the time, if ever. This means that many people have access to a lot of unused computer power. Golem's vision is to create a system for people to securely "rent" their unused computer power to people who need it to perform high-level computations. Things like rendering graphics, for example, take a lot of computer power- the more complex the job, the more expensive it becomes, eventually requiring access to resources that can be prohibitive in many situations.

Instead of needing to go to a fancy studio to render a complex set of graphics, or having to access a professional infrastructure to process a large amount of data, Golem's goal is to create on-demand access to large amounts of computer power through a distributed network- with lots of participants contributing resources to one task. Transactions happen using smart contracts and payment happens in the Golem token. Ethereum's secure blockchain infrastructure opens the door to projects like this to develop.

Another example of a project using the Ethereum backbone is BAT or Basic Attention Token. This is a new platform for digital advertising under development by the creator of JavaScript and the co-founder of Mozilla. BAT uses its own privacy-focused web browser to track user attention anonymously, keeping private information secure and sending anonymous information back to advertisers.

Users can choose to opt-in and be shown targeted ads, and they will be rewarded with BAT for their attention. Advertisers, in turn, are rewarded with BAT based on how much engagement their ads receive. By managing all of this information on a secure blockchain, the creators of BAT suggest that the capacity for fraudulent or malicious advertising is greatly reduced, the privacy of consumers is protected, and the efficiency of ad targeting is greatly improved.

Golem and BAT are two examples of very different projects utilizing their own tokens, both of which are built on the Ethereum framework. Of course, there are many more "dApps" out there, and undoubtedly many more that will be developed in the near future as Ethereum continues to gain traction and break into the mainstream.

The possibilities for deploying smart contracts on the blockchain are virtually limitless, particularly as the infrastructure for implementing blockchain-based systems develops. For example, let's pretend you owned an amusement park. For years, you've been selling tickets that can be used for various rides, games, and snacks. People buy a certain number of tickets at a kiosk before they enter the park, and then they use tickets for everything inside.

Instead of selling tickets, you could create your own token through Ethereum. Customers could download an app, buy tokens, and access rides automatically. If someone was out of tokens, they couldn't access the ride without buying more, which they could do easily from the app. With a secure blockchain system, nobody could claim to lose tickets, have tickets stolen, or sneak on to rides.

The amusement park example may be a bit silly, but the same concept could be applied to many more serious contexts. For example, the government in Dubai is making use of Ethereum in its stated goal of becoming the first blockchain-powered government by the year 2020.

Dubai has estimated, thus far, that it can save $1.5 billion dollars simply by optimizing document processing through implementing a blockchain system.

Many other governments, including Japan, China, and the US have expressed interest in exploring blockchain technology to streamline government services. In Ukraine, a startup company using the Ethereum platform was contracted in 2017 to pilot test a new property management system.

The blockchain revolution is undoubtedly underway, and Ethereum is a major player, leading the way in many sectors. From an investment perspective, many people see a lot of potential in Ethereum and decentralized blockchain applications. Before deciding whether to invest in Ethereum or an Ethereum-based project, it is a good idea to explore some of the potential downsides in addition to the promising elements.

CHAPTER 10
THE ETHEREUM ENTERPRISE ALLIANCE (EEA)

Given the surge of enthusiasm directed towards blockchain and cryptocurrencies in 2017, it should come as no surprise that a number of Fortune 500 companies have begun to explore these technologies. In March of 2017, a non-profit organization called The Ethereum Enterprise Alliance (EEA) was launched. The EEA is comprised of a variety of start-ups, think tanks, Fortune 500 companies, and others working with the Ethereum framework.

The vision of the EEA is focused primarily on the development of "private" Ethereum-based blockchains designed for enterprise environments. Unlike public blockchains, so-called "private" blockchains would not be visible or accessible to anyone. These in-house blockchains would require permission to access. Many within the larger blockchain community see this move as counterintuitive, as much of the appeal of blockchain architecture is related precisely to the fact that it is decentralized, open, and eliminates the need for trust in a third party. Skeptics have raised the question of how "private blockchains" will differ, fundamentally, from intranets. This remains to be seen.

That being said, the EEA has gained a huge amount of support throughout the early months of its existence. Many big name members are investing substantially in the development of "private blockchains," including companies like IBM, JP Morgan, Microsoft, Intel, and Deloitte. How will corporate adoption of blockchain technology impact the vision of open, decentralized, peer-to-peer exchanges? This is one question that looms large in the minds of many independent investors and those who see the possibilities for blockchain technology to create systemic change and re-imagine institutional structures.

CHAPTER 11
CRITICISMS, RISKS & CHALLENGES CONCERNING ETHEREUM

Any new technology faces obstacles and challenges as it moves into the real world, and Ethereum is no exception. While there is enthusiastic support, an active community and obvious potential surrounding Ethereum, anybody who wants to get involved should also be aware that challenges and risks exist, as well.

Because the Ethereum platform is open and accessible, many companies and projects have sprung up around the Ethereum ecosystem, building projects on the Ethereum blockchain. In the long run, this is probably a good thing. When we consider the big picture and remember that we are still in the early stages of exploring this technology, a diverse group of initial developers competing to create decentralized applications will, in theory, ultimately strengthen the Ethereum platform.

In the short term, however, this climate has led to a huge surge in "ICO's," or Initial Coin Offerings. ICO's are a largely unregulated way for companies to raise capital for a new cryptocurrency-based project. A form of crowd-funding, ICO's typically sell a percentage of a new cryptocurrency or token to a group of early investors in exchange for some other form of legal tender, usually Bitcoin. This method of fundraising gives startups a way to bypass many of the stringent regulations involved in raising venture capital or borrowing from banks through the traditional means. This is very similar to IPO's selling shares of a company to raise money for future plans or operations, except in this case rather than buying stock an investor would buy virtual currency.

For investors, buying in early to a promising project can have a lot of appeal. If the project is successful, the value of the associated currency will increase, thus potentially giving them a sizeable profit. Because ICO's are unregulated by financial authorities like the SEC (Securities Exchange Commission), however, there is a risk of fraudulent ICO scams.

While ICO's can be very successful and lucrative ventures, this can be a high-risk space. Particularly considering that anyone can issue their own currency fairly easily with Ethereum, it is important to perform due diligence as an investor. You can't swing a cat in cyberspace without hitting an ICO developing a new Ethereum-based application that promises to make early investors into millionaires.

Beyond the potential for fraud, there are some other potential concerns that come with the ICO model as it relates to Ethereum. In many cases, early investors in a promising project are actually companies rather than private individuals. One result of the ICO model in the Ethereum space is that we end up with *companies* holding a lot of Ether, rather than individuals, per se. In terms of Ether as a currency, it is important to consider the implications of having large amounts of Ether tied up in companies.

Simply put, companies have expenses. They need to pay employees, pay for office space, marketing, etc. What if one big company has a successful funding round, gains a lot of Ether from investors, and then doesn't really develop anything that great? That company still needs to pay its expenses. Perhaps they dump all of their Ether at once and cash out. Sizeable "dumps" like this affect the price of any currency, and if one big company dumps, others may see the price drop, become alarmed, and begin to dump their holdings as well, thus snowballing into a huge price drop that ultimately screws individual investors the most.

This is not necessarily an inevitable scenario, and it is certainly not a potential problem that is exclusive to Ethereum, but it is one concern that arises when a handful of large companies hold a considerable amount of Ether.

As a potential investor, it is always a good idea to do your own research. Read white papers, engage in discussions, and determine for yourself whether or not you think a project is solid. Marketing and hype can play a big role in this space, and following the crowd into the ICO flavor-of-the-month is often far more likely to end up in a loss than a profit.

One of the biggest concerns from voices within the broader Ethereum community is the way that third-party applications may impact the underlying Ethereum platform. This applies to the potential for fraudulent ICO's to issue a scam currency using Ethereum's infrastructure, but it can also apply to well-intentioned efforts.

We know that Ethereum is a platform for building decentralized applications. We know, also, that part of the appeal of the Ethereum platform is the capacity to execute applications on a blockchain. The potential for this vision is very exciting, but baked into the reality of actually building dApps on the Ethereum platform is the fact that writing software is hard.

Finding developers who can write good, bug-free software for Android or iOS can be difficult even though those are hugely popular platforms upon which many applications are built. When it comes to developing applications for the Ethereum blockchain, finding developers who can write code in the Solidity language, or other languages being used to implement smart contracts, can be even more challenging. In fact, many very good programmers today have never even heard of Ethereum!

As the demand for developers who can write code in the Solidity language continues to grow, there is an opportunity for aspiring programmers to find work in this field and comparatively little competition. While there are definitely some talented programmers working with Ethereum, it is important to remember that "smart contracts" have only existed for a few years, and therefore even talented programmers may have relatively little experience with this type of software development.

Naturally, any new technology will go through a similar process in its early days. When considering Ethereum, however, it is important to think about the impact that potential vulnerabilities in applications built on the Ethereum blockchain might have on Ether as a currency. If one or more applications built on the Ethereum platform suffers from a significant hack or is full of bugs, how will that affect the value of Ether?

It is impossible to predict the future, but for a potential investor, it is a good idea to think seriously about how third-party applications built on the Ethereum platform might impact the perception of the platform itself, and subsequently the value of Ether. Of course, large-scale adoption and a series of successful dApps running on Ethereum could impact the value of Ether in a positive way, and that is clearly the direction in which serious investors believe the project to be heading. (Otherwise, one can assume, they would not be serious investors).

CHAPTER 12
GETTING STARTED WITH ETHEREUM

If you feel as though you would like to learn about the nuts and bolts of Ethereum, or are thinking of hiring someone to create an Ethereum based application, then exploring this chapter will be beneficial.

If not, we suggest you skip this chapter and come back to it at a time you feel that it will become more relevant to you.

To start using the Ethereum platform one will need a specific piece of software – AKA a client – that is able to run contracts and network with other computers using specific protocols.

There are multiple clients written in different languages, which helps to broaden support for the network and gives choice to programmers with various strengths.

As with most projects, it helps to have multiple teams to implement the protocols at this tends to make them more reliable and robust – using cross reference checks and various tried and tested checking methods.

There are several clients that run on top of the wallet, offering additional features, the more notable of which were compiled by CoinDesk and are outlined below:

- **Ethereum (J).** A Java version.

- **EthereumH.** A version was written in the Haskell programming language.

- **Go-ethereum.** Written in Google's Go language, this is currently the most popular ethereum client. Commonly called "geth", it includes a mining component while allowing users the ability to create contracts and transfer funds between addresses

- **Parity.** A low-footprint version written in a language called Rust, spawned by Mozilla.

- **Pyethapp.** A Python implementation that includes mining and virtual machine capabilities. This has been subcontracted to a team at Brainbot, led by Heiko Hees.

- **Ruby-Ethereum.** A version was written in the Ruby web application programming language.

- **Cpp ethereum.** Led by Christian Reitwiessner, cpp ethereum is a C++ client.

Ethereumjs-lib. An implementation in JavaScript

If you are not comfortable working in command line, there is a simple tutorial on **http://ethereum.org/token** that will help you create a token. There are also step-by-step instructions on how to implement a contract via that token.

Once you're more familiar, Christian Reitwiessner has elaborated on the developing social ethics and best practices of smart contract development in **public presentations**.

Learning Solidity

To begin with, having a solid basis in JavaScript will be extremely helpful in learning Solidity.

If you are not comfortable working in command line, there is a simple tutorial on:

http://ethereum.org/token

Whether you know JavaScript or not, here is a list of resources you can use to learn more about coding in Solidity:

Solidity Documentation – The most comprehensive resource for Solidity, this tutorial is geared toward people familiar with programming, but who may not have experience with ethereum or blockchain technology in general.

Ether.fund – This online resource maintains a list of example Solidity contracts that can be a useful resource for developing your own contracts or understanding how different methods of creating contracts work.

Ethereum Github Wiki – A community maintained a wiki for the technology, this resource contains a list of resources for dapp developers that will be most useful for those with some programming background. These include tools, code examples, development environments and technical references.

ConsenSys – If you are new to programming and the ethereum blockchain, you might find this "Intro to Programming Smart Contracts" by ethereum startup ConsenSys useful. It introduces basic concepts in dapp development and walks the reader through one possible dapp development workflow.

Ledger Labs – Another "Intro to Dapp Development" tutorial is available from Canada-based blockchain consultancy Ledger Labs. While a work in progress, it currently walks the reader through installing Geth, running a local node, a basic contract design and a more advanced auction contract example.

If you are completely new to programming, you might find that you need to first learn the basic concepts involved in any coding.

Online interactive platform Codeacademy has **free interactive tutorials** that will teach you the basics of JavaScript, the language on which Solidity is based. While the details and syntax are different, many of the basic concepts you will learn are still applicable in Solidity.

CHAPTER 13
THE FUTURE OF ETHEREUM, DECENTRALIZED APPLICATIONS & BLOCKCHAIN TECHNOLOGY

The value of Ether reached record highs in 2017, and many speculate that the value will continue to trend upwards over time. Many major companies have adopted the Ethereum vision of a flexible blockchain platform with the ability to utilize smart contracts. As the promise of blockchain technology becomes clearer on a global scale, a surge of entrepreneurs has emerged seeking to integrate this technology into every field from energy to healthcare to politics.

Whether the Ethereum platform will ultimately become the definitive framework for building decentralized blockchain applications remains to be seen. It is possible that Ethereum is akin to an early web browser like NetScape Navigator and that some future effort will become the "Google of blockchain." Considering how new this technology is, it would be naïve not to consider that possibility. Of course, it is also conceivable that Ethereum will continue to grow, improve, and ultimately dominate this space. The upcoming update to using the Casper algorithm and the Proof-of-Stake model will serve as one test in terms of Ethereum's ability to evolve.

Whether you plan to invest in Ether, another token issued through an Ethereum-based application, or you are interested in building your own dApp on the

Ethereum blockchain, it is important to stay informed. Technology changes in this space incredibly quickly, and as blockchain enters major industries, we will likely begin to see changes in terms of how cryptocurrencies and blockchain applications are regulated. Joining online communities and conversations, such as Reddit, Slack channels, and via Twitter are a great way to stay current on developments in the Ethereum platform. Learning about other platforms, reading whitepapers, and becoming familiar with the leading thinkers in this field is a good way to develop a deeper understanding and broader perspective, which can help you formulate your own opinions about what technologies are likely to succeed and how to invest and participate.

How the future will play out is, of course, something that we cannot foresee. Whatever the future looks like, however, it is almost certainly going to be shaped by blockchain technology. Today, Ethereum offers one of the most well-established and innovative approaches to making this technology accessible, flexible, and exciting. For investors, developers, and entrepreneurs in this cutting-edge space, the possibilities are unlimited.

CONCLUSION

I'd like to thank you for purchasing this book and I commend you for taking the time to learn about Ethereum.

I hope this short read was able to help you to get a basic understanding of exactly what Ethereum is, sparking your interest to do some further research and start your journey toward sovereignty.

The next step is to get active on the message forums and with the resources mentioned in this book.

Finally, if you enjoyed this book then I'd like to ask if you would be kind enough to leave a review on Amazon.

It will be highly appreciated.

Thank you and good luck!

© **Copyright 2017 by – Artemis Caro - All rights reserved.**

This document is geared towards providing exact and reliable information in regards to the topic and issue covered. The publication is sold with the idea that the publisher is not required to render accounting, officially permitted, or otherwise, qualified services. If advice is necessary, legal or professional, a practiced individual in the profession should be ordered.

- From a Declaration of Principles which was accepted and approved equally by a Committee of the American Bar Association and a Committee of Publishers and Associations.

In no way is it legal to reproduce, duplicate, or transmit any part of this document in either electronic means or in printed format. Recording of this publication is strictly prohibited and any storage of this document is not allowed unless with written permission from the publisher. All rights reserved.

The information provided herein is stated to be truthful and consistent, in that any liability, in terms of inattention or otherwise, by any usage or abuse of any policies, processes, or directions contained within is the solitary and utter responsibility of the recipient reader. Under no circumstances will any legal responsibility or blame be held against the publisher or author for any reparation, damages, or monetary loss due to the information herein, either directly or indirectly.

Respective authors own all copyrights not held by the publisher.

The information herein is offered for informational purposes solely, and is universal as so. The presentation of the information is without contract or any type of guarantee assurance.

The trademarks that are used are without any consent, and the publication of the trademark is without permission or backing by the trademark owner. All trademarks and brands within this book are for clarifying purposes only and are the owned by the owners themselves, not affiliated with this document.

www.ingramcontent.com/pod-product-compliance
Lightning Source LLC
Chambersburg PA
CBHW050021230526
45470CB00003B/1066